BASKETBALL
RULES IN
PICTURES

Edited by
A. G. Jacobs

Revised and illustrated by
Michael Brown

Book Consultant:
Patrick McKee

A Perigee Book

A Perigee Book
Published by The Berkley Publishing Group
200 Madison Avenue
New York, NY 10016

Published simultaneously in Canada
First Perigee edition: October 1985
Revised edition, first printing: October 1993

Library of Congress Cataloging-in-Publication Data

Basketball rules in pictures / originally edited by A. G. Jacobs;
   completely revised and updated by Michael Brown;
   illustrated by Michael Brown.
        p.   cm.
    ISBN 0-399-51842-8
     1. Basketball—Rules—Juvenile literature.
  I. Jacobs, A. G. (A. Gertrude) II. Brown, Michael.
  GV885.45.B395   1993   93-30306 CIP AC
  796.323'02'022—dc20

Front cover photograph © by Brian Drake/SportsChrome East-West

Printed in the United States of America
      9   10   11   12   13   14   15   16   17   18   19   20

This book is printed on acid-free paper.

Table of Contents

Introduction

A good understanding of the rules of basketball makes playing and watching basketball a lot more fun. If you want to enjoy the sport to its utmost, whether you are a player or a fan, this book is for you.

The rules of basketball, like those of most sports, have two purposes. One is to protect the players, the other to prevent tactics that might interfere with the action and balance that make the game exciting. We have tried here to explain the rules in the context of the game—to stress the spirit rather than the letter of the law, hoping to present knowledge that is both useful and memorable to players. The emphasis is on common occurrences rather than complex points of a rule for uncommon events such as, for example, a flagrant false double technical foul.

The rules explained in this book are based on men's NCAA rules. They will apply to most games played by junior high, high school, and college basketball teams in the U.S., with only slight variations for women's play. However, every conference has minor rule variations (the length of the halves, for example, or the number of personal fouls allowed) that are designed to accommodate the maturity

and ability levels of the players they serve. Let's face it, the ACME Appliance Aces in the local recreation league are not the Chicago Bulls. The games of such different teams will not, and should not, be administered the same way. Junior high kids probably are not ready for 40 minutes of basketball plus overtime. League administrators will make—and players should expect—reasonable adjustments for their particular situation.

Young players should concentrate primarily on developing playing skills, not becoming basketball lawyers. But when the action is hottest and fastest, it is the superior player *who stays within the rules* who will triumph, as the 1993 men's NCAA tournament proved. The best players know the rules so well that they are second nature.

Games can be lost, players injured, and friendships strained because of ignorance or disregard for the rules. This is sad and ironic, since basketball has one of the most simple and fair sets of playing rules that exist in team sports. We hope that this book will spread greater knowledge and enjoyment of those rules and of the sport of basketball.

5

Chapter 1

The Court and Equipment

Basketball doesn't rely as heavily on equipment as, say, football. But the court and equipment that is used must meet certain requirements. Your league probably mirrors the NCAA, which gives exact measurements in feet and inches of the required dimensions of the court, all areas in it, and of the equipment. Two noticeable exceptions are that the three-point line is farther out on pro courts than on other courts, and the actual length of the high school and junior high school courts is often ten feet shorter than NCAA courts.

THE COURT

Endlines and sidelines
The diagram of the court shows lengths for the endlines and sidelines. It is the *inside edge* of the line that marks in-bounds and out-of-bounds. In other words, if you dribble the ball on the line, the ball is out of bounds. Also, if the ball handler steps on the line, he or she will be called out.

Other areas
The **three-point field goal line** should be marked at each end of the court. If you want to practice three-pointers at home, you could mark one off on your court. It should be a semicircle, with a radius that measures 19 feet, 9 inches from the center of the basket to the outside of the semicircle. The pro three-point arc is 23 feet, 9 inches from the hoop. The diagram shows other areas of the court that must be clearly marked. These include the **center jump circle, central division line, free throw lane,** and **free throw line.** The purposes and restrictions regarding these areas will be explained later when we cover the playing rules.

Restraining lines
If you look around the court you'll notice a sort of buffer zone immediately outside the sidelines and endlines of the official playing area. This area should be clearly marked by a restraining line. The restraining line recommended by the NCAA is a dashed line, two inches wide, of 12-inch segments alternating with 12-inch spaces. Fans, photographers, or parents should not be sitting or standing with their toes on the edge of the court, where they might distract the players, interfere with the play, or be injured. They should stay behind the restraining line.

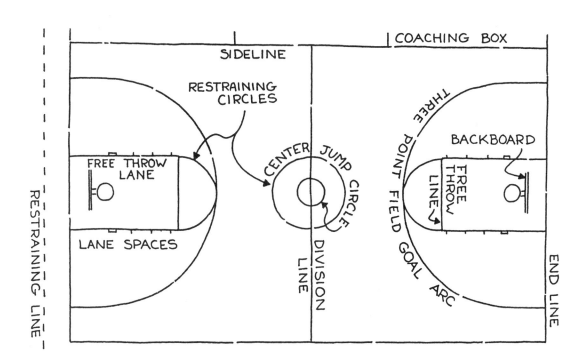

The restraining line at the sidelines should keep people back an absolute minimum of three feet. If at all possible in the physical space allowed, six feet is better and ten feet is the ideal buffer zone. The restraining line at the endline should keep folks back six feet from the end of the court. These buffer zones are necessary for the safety of the both players and spectators.

Finally, **the ceiling** above the court should be at least 25 feet high, higher if possible. The whole court should be well and evenly lighted. That means if your cheerleaders hang banners in the gym, they should be up high and out of the way of the possible flight of the ball and the lights.

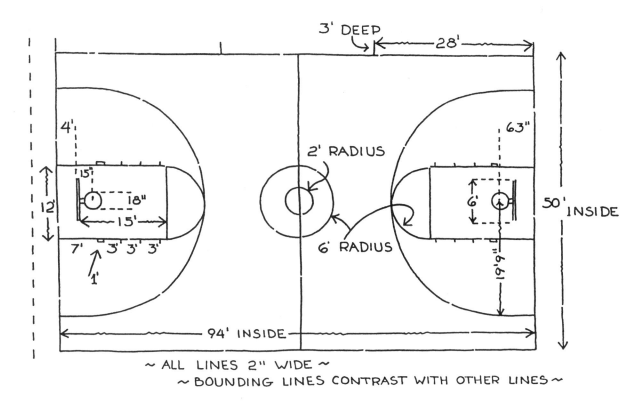

~ ALL LINES 2" WIDE ~
~ BOUNDING LINES CONTRAST WITH OTHER LINES ~

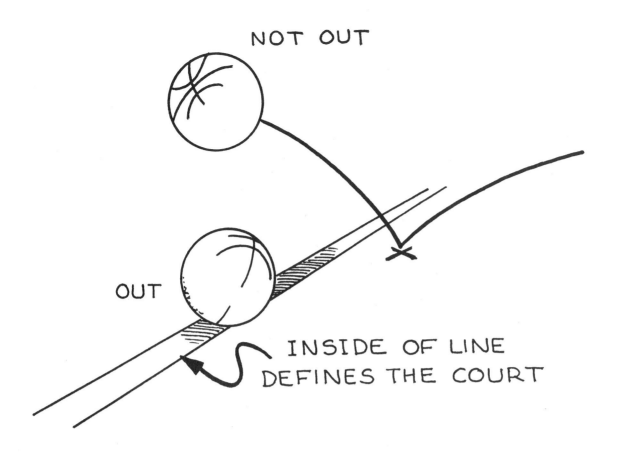

NOT OUT

OUT

INSIDE OF LINE
DEFINES THE COURT

OUT OF BOUNDS

In general, whether you are in bounds or out of bounds is decided by where you are contacting the floor. Your contact with the floor also determines whether you are in the frontcourt or the backcourt. Your in/out status when you are in the air is determined by where you last touched the floor. Similarly, when the ball touches an official, whether or not the ball will be called out is determined by where the official is standing on the court—in or out of bounds.

It's important for players to remember that the lines that mark the free throw lane are part of the lane, but the marks for the lane spaces that separate opposing rebounders and the semicircular area around the foul line are not part of the lane.

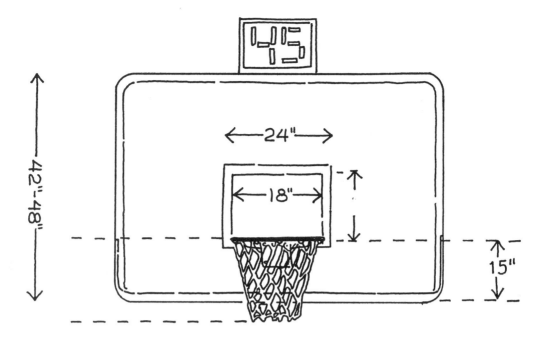

The Basket and Backboard

Now let's look at the basket.

The position of the basket and its height are obviously critical matters. Any change, even a small one, will throw everyone's shooting off. The top edge of the rim should be 10 feet from the floor. The rim should be 6 inches away from the board and the plane of the rim should be parallel to the floor. The inside diameter of the basket rim should be 18 inches and the net should hang down from the rim about 15 to 18 inches.

The basket should be attached securely to the backboard; it should be secure enough to stay put even if the backboard shatters. Rims that flex are okay so long as the ball rebounds off them just like the unmovable ones. Rims like this, equipped with a pressure release mechanism, should be able to support 230 pounds before they tilt. If they do tilt, they should automatically return to position after the player lets go.

Today, the standard NCAA backboard is rectangular and is made of a rigid, transparent material. They should be 6 feet wide and 3 1/2 feet long; backboards in many older gyms are often four feet long, and that's acceptable. A red light is often positioned behind the backboard to indicate that the time has expired on the shot clock.

The sides and bottom of the backboard should be padded with an impact-absorbing material. In reality, a court that is used exclusively by young—and therefore shorter—players may not have this padding.

The support system for the backboard should be at least 8 feet behind the board and its horizontal parts should be at least 7 feet above floor level. This is to keep a player who is concentrating on a lay-up in heavy traffic from completing the move to the basket with a bash into a steel girder. The backboard must be centered between the sidelines. It should be 4 feet inside and parallel to the court's endline.

THE BALL

NCAA basketballs must be "basketball orange" with the characteristic pebbly surface. The outer surface of the ball must be leather unless both teams okay a ball made of another material. Balls normally are supplied by the home team, but if the referee says the ones they have aren't up to standard, then the ref can designate that a ball belonging to the visitors be used.

All the basketballs used in a game should have uniform air pressure so that they all have about the same bounce. A ball should be stamped with the air pressure that it needs to give it the legal bounce. To check your ball, drop it from 6 feet; it should bounce up from 49 to 54 inches.

The ball should be perfectly round and balanced. If it is, when you dribble with no spin, the ball will return directly to your hand.

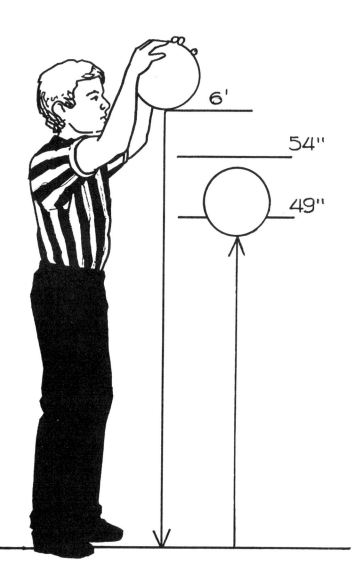

STANDARD BALL MEASUREMENTS

Men's Basketball:
Seams: not wider than 1/4 inch
Circumference: between 29.5 and 30 inches
Weight: 20 to 22 ounces for men's

Women's Basketball:
Seams: not wider than 1/8 inch
Circumference: between 28.5 and 29 inches
Weight: 18 to 20 ounces

THE SCOREBOARD, GAME CLOCK, AND SHOT CLOCK

Since all basketball competitions must have visible scoreboards and game-clocks, your gym probably has a scoreboard and clock somewhere up on a wall. Having a backup clock and scoreboard is a good idea in case of breakdowns—especially during championship tournaments.

At the NCAA level, a shot clock is also required. It must be visible to its operator and to the players. If possible, the shot clock should be in a recess directly above the backboard, to the left of the basket. If you need one and this won't work on your particular court, the shot clock could be on the floor at each end of the court. Again, a backup should be available in case of a breakdown.

Finally, a team-possession arrow must be visible to show which team gets the ball if the alternate-possession rule is applied during the game.

The benches for each team should be on either side of, and the same distance from, the official scorer's table so both of the coaches and each team's substitutes have equal access when checking into the game or when a coach asks a question.

Each bench should also have a coaching box marked on the floor in front of the bench. It should be 3 feet deep and at least 28 feet long, or as long as the bench. In high school, this box is smaller, only 6 feet long. This area gives the coaching staff room to move and talk to the players on the bench, but is also there to remind them in their exuberance not to interfere with the game.

The visitors always get to choose the basket where they will practice before the game, and this is always the one they shoot at for the first half. Traditionally, this is the basket opposite the bench they are sitting on so they will be shooting at the basket nearest their bench at the end of the game.

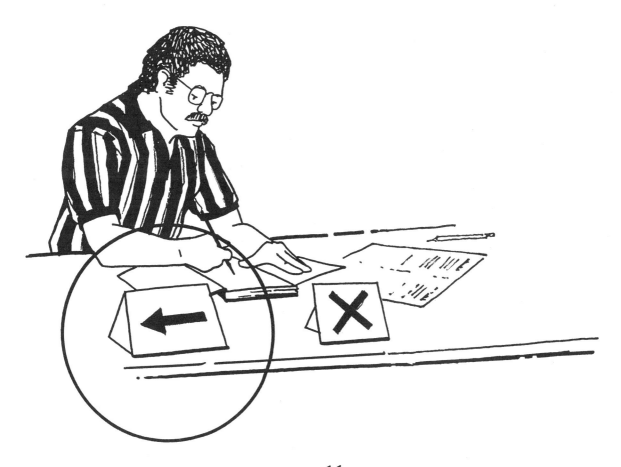

GARMENTS AND NUMBERS

Players' garments must allow the referees to quickly and accurately identify each player. Make sure the numbers are visible and easy to read at a glance. They must be at least 6 inches high on the back and 4 inches on the front.

All members of the same team must wear the same color on fronts and backs, and customarily the home team wears jerseys that are predominantly white. Your uniforms should be free of distracting decorations. NCAA rules, for instance, spell out how many inches wide the stripes on the uniforms may be, and what kind of logos, decorations, and numbers are allowed. Of course, most rec leagues allow team sponsors (the local auto dealer who gives $500 for uniforms, for example) to have their names or a little advertising on the shirts.

Your shirts should be the kind that can be tucked in. College players must tuck theirs in, and of course it looks better—so tuck 'em in. What your undershirts and undertights may look like if they are visible is also covered in the rules—so if you're prone to catching a cold and planning to wear an undershirt beneath your jersey, make sure it matches your teammates' gear and the team uniform.

Also, if you want to have uniforms like those of the major college programs, don't display more than two identifying names, which might be the school, mascot, player's name, sponsor, and so on. NCAA uniforms should have no more than three colors in all, including colors used for numbers and piping.

LEGAL NUMBERS

The legal numbers that can be used for players' numbers are:

    0, 3, 4, 5, 00,
    10 through 15,
    20 through 25,
    30 through 35,
    40 through 45, and
    50 through 55.

This list of numbers is not arbitrary. A referee often signals a player's number to the scorekeeper by flashing the fingers on one hand. If your number is 22, for instance, the ref would hold up two fingers, then two again. And of course, one hand can't show any number greater than five. The numbers 1 and 2 can't be used as a player's number because they are used in signaling to the scorer the number of shots being awarded in a free throw situation.

Obviously, you and a teammate can't use the same number, so if both of you have the same lucky number, you'll just have to flip for it at the beginning of the season.

DANGEROUS EQUIPMENT

During play, you aren't allowed to wear or use *anything* that might endanger the other players. This includes any kind of hand guard, brace, or cast worn at or below the elbow, even if padded. On your upper arms, shoulders, and legs, you can wear guards or braces, but they must be well covered with protective padding. If you wear a knee brace, make sure that it is properly covered. If you're wearing a guard for a broken nose, it must be padded, and so should any protector you wear for your eyeglasses.

Wearing jewelry is not allowed. It can give nasty cuts or knock a tooth out. Also, no headgear is allowed, except soft sweatbands that are less than 2 inches wide.

Chapter 2

Officials and Their Duties

Every game must have at least one referee and one umpire; the umpire has similar duties to and is supervised by the referee. Having two umpires is better, but most high schools and junior highs are lucky if they can get one of each. If possible, backup timers and scorekeepers should also be present, and one shot-clock operator. If only one scorer and one timer are available, it's important that they know what they are doing. Normally, the timers and scorers share a table at the sideline. Remember, they are officials and should be treated with the same level of respect you show the referee.

This chapter highlights what the officials may do, must do, and should not do. One thing is universally true: Officials may not waive an official rule or interpretation for any period of time during play. In other words, they don't make the rules, they are the ones who try to enforce them.

THE REFEREE

BEFORE THE GAME

The responsibilities of the officials actually begin, and they can make rulings, before the game starts. Officials come on duty half an hour before game time. Before the start of play, the referee is supposed to make sure the gym meets the league standards and that everything used for the game—court balls, clocks, lighting, signals, backboards, and so on—is in working order.

Also beginning 15 minutes before game time, the officials may call infractions that take place on or off the court. If a player or coach, for instance, should begin to abuse the referee for something that took place in an earlier game, or dunk the ball during warm ups, it doesn't matter that play hasn't started yet. The offender can be charged with a technical foul. Officials may also call infractions during times when the play has been temporarily stopped.

It's the referee's responsibility to let each team know when there are only three minutes remaining until the start of the game and the second half. It's the ref who tosses the ball to start the game, and any overtime period.

Fouls

To call a foul, the official blows the whistle to stop play and signal the timekeeper to stop the clock. He makes sure the scorers know who the offender was, and shows with his fingers how many free throws there will be, if any.

If it is not a shooting foul, but instead entitles one team to a throw-in, the official points out the spot where the throw-in should be made and hands the ball to the player who will throw it.

When some disagreement or dispute arises between officials, the referee decides the outcome. But

remember, while it is his (or her) job to settle disputes or discrepancies between umpires, timers, and scorers, *settling a dispute* is not the same as *overriding a decision*. No official, not even the ref, may set aside rulings made by other officials in their own areas of responsibility. For instance, the ref may not correct the judgment of an umpire who calls a ball out, but may correct a misinterpretation of the rules.

The referee rules on any dispute or on anything else that takes place that is not specifically covered in the rules. The ref also has the final say on whether a basket counts.

Correctable errors

Sometimes officials do make errors; although the referee may not override the *judgment* of another official, it is possible to amend certain kinds of errors. For example:

- a free throw that should have been awarded but wasn't, or a free throw that was awarded but should not have been;

- a free throw taken by the wrong player; or

- a score that was incorrectly allowed or incorrectly canceled.

To be corrected, these mistakes must be pointed out to an official before the ball becomes live again and the clock is started. If this officiating error was made by the official while the clock was still running, then it must be corrected by an official before the ball becomes live again after the clock stops the next time.

When play is interrupted to correct one of these mistakes, the clock will resume running at the point when play was stopped, not back at the point where the error was made.

Video replay

In basketball, it is very rare that video is replayed to help make a ruling. There are only a few cases where the league offices may do so to settle a protest:

- a scoring or timing error;

- in case of a malfunctioning clock; or

- to assess the involvement of players in a fight.

Video replays *cannot* be used to help determine fouls, basket interference, goaltending, or the release of the ball when the horn sounds. The officials make these decisions, and theirs is the final word. This helps keep the game moving and eliminates a lot of second guessing of officials.

Official score

At the end of each half, the referee will officially okay the score. When the ref leaves the court after the game is finished, the final score becomes official—and the responsibilities of the ref and other officials are considered to be finished.

THE JOB OF THE SCORERS

The official scorer keeps a book at the scorer's table. They keep a record of the score, of course, and also of the players' names and numbers and a record of who starts and who substitutes. They must let the referee know about any discrepancy in these records.

THE LINEUP

At least ten minutes before play is set to begin, each team must deliver to the scorers certain information about their lineup:

- the names and numbers of all eligible squad members; and

- the five starting players.

If this information is not delivered, your team may receive a technical foul. Your team could also get a technical foul for adding names at the last second, changing a player's number without reporting it, or changing the original list of starting players. However, if illness or injury causes those kind of changes at the last minute, that's okay, just clear it up with the scorer right there. (Also, a team is allowed to replace a starter before the game if they do it in order to let the new player shoot a technical-foul free throw.)

If something happens, and your team must play with fewer than five players (a flu epidemic or a late car pool, maybe), that's okay. However, if five eligible players are present and able, then five must be on the court.

Interestingly, the NCAA states in their rules that as few as two players may play as a "team" —or even one player, if the ref believes that one has a chance of winning. Michael Jordan versus Sticksville Jr. High, maybe?

During play, scorers must record a lot of information:

- number of field goals made, noting the difference between two- and three-point fieldgoals;

- number of free throws made;

- number of free throws missed;

- personal fouls called on each player;

- technical fouls called on each player;

- combinations of personal, unsporting, and contact technical fouls;

- the second technical foul for unsporting conduct called on anyone associated with a team;

- the third noncontact, technical foul called on a team member or staff member;

- anyone ejected by the referee;

- time-outs taken by each team (scorers notify a team when they take their fifth time-out); and

- the number of team fouls.

At times, the scorers need to get the attention of an official—for example, to make the referee aware that one team has committed seven fouls and the other team is now entitled to a bonus free throw or that a player has five fouls and is disqualified. To get the ref's attention, they should use some sort of bell or horn. Whatever it is, it's important that it sound quite different from the whistle being used by the referee and umpire and the horn that signals the end of the game. Also, the scorers should wait until the ball is dead to signal the official, or until it's in the hands of the team that has committed an offense. They don't want to take an advantage away from the team that did nothing wrong.

If there are two or more scorers, they should compare their records and let the referee know when there's a discrepancy.

1. SHOT CLOCK OPERATOR
2. TIMER
3. SCORER

SUBSTITUTIONS

As a substitute, you must report to the scorer's table in order to get into the game. You must give your number and the number of the player you are replacing to the scorer. The scorers should sound the horn to signal the substitution. They should signal as soon as the ball is dead.

If you're going to substitute, pay attention. Stay off the court until the referee beckons you. Then, go in immediately. But always wait until the official signals you to come in.

If you are told during a time-out to sub in, you are still responsible for reporting to the scorers. You must inform them, or be clearly headed to do so, before the 15-second signal just before the end of the time-out. Substitutions may not be initiated during that 15-second period before the time-out is over. And if a change in the lineup takes place between halves—so you're starting the second half with players different from those who left the court—someone on your team must let the scorer know, before the end-of-intermission buzzer sounds, who will be on court. The scorer's job is tough—they've got to keep track of and write down a lot of information. This rule gives them the time to avoid errors.

A sub is not officially in the game until he or she has *legally* entered the court. Subs should not enter improperly during a dead ball. If a substitute is being sent in to take your place, and then the coach wants to put you right back in, you must wait until play stops again, then resumes, and some time has run off the clock. This is to keep coaches from relaying instructions to the players without calling a time-out or making a real substitution. Substitutes are meant to *play*, if only for a short while.

FREE-THROWS

The rules don't allow players to be substituted just to take a free throw for a teammate. The only time a player will be sent in to take someone's free throw is if the free thrower is injured or disqualified. When a player who was fouled can't take a throw awarded, the substitute *must* be the one to make it. If no legal substitute is available, anyone else on the team may take the throw. In the case of a technical foul, the captain designates who will shoot it, and he may designate a newly substituted player.

THE TIMER'S JOB

It is the timer's job to start and stop the clock at the appropriate times. A timer must be paying close attention and immediately start or stop the clock:

- at the beginning and end of each half and beginning and end of each time-out;

- when there's a missed free throw and the ball stays live;

- when play starts back up with a throw-in, as soon as the ball comes in contact with any player on the court; and

- when there's a jump ball, as soon as the ball is controlled.

Some of the timer's other responsibilities are to:

- know when the halves are scheduled to start and signal the referee three minutes beforehand;

- signal fifteen seconds before the end of an intermission or a charged time-out, and give a signal when these periods are over;

- signal at the end of the halves and any extra playing periods;

- record the length of play—when play starts and finishes at the halves and at game's end; and

- record the time on the game clock when stoppages occur.

Note: The timer will not normally stop the game clock after a field goal. The ball is put immediately back into play, and those few seconds are allowed to elapse on the clock. However, in the *last minute* of play, the clock *is* stopped and restarted after the ball is live again.

NCAA games have time-outs that are 75 seconds long. The referee should signal that play is to resume at once when the signal sounds.

If the timer fails to stop or start the clock correctly, it's the referee's job to figure out the discrepancy as best he or she can and correct the error.

THE SHOT-CLOCK OPERATOR

NCAA rules state that a team must attempt to score within a stipulated length of time. When your team gets the ball—whether through play on the court or by a throw-in—you've got 35 seconds to take a shot at the basket in a men's game, 30 seconds in a women's game. The shot-clock operator times it.

When a team holds the ball longer than 35 seconds without a shot hitting the rim of the basket, the shot-clock operator will sound a horn or buzzer. The referee will signal a violation and the other team will get the ball. This violation is not official unless the device sounds and an official acknowledges the signal.

During play, when possession of the ball changes, the shot-clock operator restarts the shot clock as soon as one team has established control of the ball. The shot clock is reset after a defensive foul or a shot that hits the rim but misses—if the same team that shot rebounds the ball, they begin a new 35-second period.

The shot clock is *not* reset for loose ball or a held ball. Remember, if the other team knocks the ball loose, and there is a scramble for the ball, the shot clock keeps running, so if you get the ball back you may be running out of time and have to force a shot. The clock is reset with a new 35-second period when there is a defensive foul or violations and when a shot strikes the basket ring, whether it makes it through or not. The clock also stops and continues without being reset when play resumes after a time-out, after a defensive player knocks it out of bounds, or after a player is hurt (or loses a contact lens).

It's okay for the shot-clock operator to turn the clock off when it shows more time than the game clock. You can't, after all, hold the ball more than 35 seconds if there's only 12 seconds left in the game. If there's overtime, the game and shot clocks are reset.

TALKING TO OFFICIALS

There's little place in basketball for lengthy dialogue between coaches and officials. The coach may get clarification from the scorer's table, but should try to keep communication to a minimum. But such communication is necessary at times. The captain of the team is the one who should speak to an official regarding an interpretation of the rules or to obtain what the NCAA rules call "essential information." But *any* player on the court may ask an official for a time-out. In all cases, anyone associated with a team should address the officials courteously.

Chapter 3

Starting and Stopping Play

PLAY PERIOD

A basketball game is divided into two 20-minute halves, with a 15-minute break, the halftime, between these two periods.

The game starts with a jump ball (see below) at center court. The second half begins with the ball being thrown in from midcourt by the team that is entitled to it according to the alternate-possession arrow (see below). To start overtime periods, the official tosses a jump ball just like at the start of the first half.

JUMP BALL

If you are one of the two players jumping for the ball, you must have at least one of your feet on or inside your half of the jump circle in the center of the court. Your half of the circle is the one farther from your own basket. Both your feet must be inside the larger restraining circle. The official is supposed to toss up the ball exactly between the two of you and higher than either of you can jump; you are allowed to tap the ball when it's at its highest point or on the way down. If it touches the floor without either of you touching it, the official must stop play and toss the ball again.

You've both got to stay in the outer jump-ball circle until the ball has been tapped by one of you. The rules don't compel you to actually jump. Maybe your opponent is a foot taller than you and you figure your time is better spent moving to cover another opponent—but don't overdo it. You must stay in the circle until it is tapped. Also, you're not allowed to catch the ball, or to tap it more than twice.

The other eight players on the court during the jump ball are not allowed to touch the larger restraining circle. They may also not jostle or shift positions when the official is ready to toss the ball, nor may they take positions next to a teammate if an opponent wants to be in between them.

DEAD BALL

Play is temporarily stopped when the ball becomes dead.

Some of the reasons the ball becomes dead are:

- a player makes a basket;

- a player fails to make a free throw for a technical foul;

- a player fails to make the first of two free throws to be taken;

- there's a held ball;

- the ball lodges on the basket support structure;

- an official blows the whistle for a foul, floor or free throw violation, or any other reason; or

- time runs out.

ALTERNATING POSSESSION

In past years, many dead-ball situations (see above) called for a jump ball to get the ball back in play. These days, rather than taking the time to set up and restart play with a jump ball, the teams alternate throwing the ball in. An arrow at the scorer's table indicates whose turn it is to throw the ball in.

When such a situation occurs, the team who did not win control of the ball from the jump ball that started the game gets the first of these alternate-possession throw-ins. If you are to throw the ball in, move quickly to the sidelines close to the spot where the ball was ruled dead. The official should indicate the throw-in spot to you.

NCAA rules specify the situations where, when the ball becomes dead, the alternate-possession rule should be used. Notice one thing the infractions have in common is that they were committed by both teams or by neither teams—neither team is more at fault than the other. Use the alternating-possession rule when:

- the ball is held between two opponents;

- the ball is sent out of bounds by opponents who touch it at the same time;

- there are simultaneous personal or technical fouls by opponents;

- the ball goes out and the officials are not sure or don't agree about who last touched the ball; or

- a dead ball that was caused by neither team—for example, if the ball becomes deflated during play.

STOPPING THE CLOCK

Here are some of the reasons that cause the game and the shot clock to be stopped:

- an official signals a foul or violation;

- an official grants a player's request for a time-out;

- an official signals a held ball or other alternating-possession situation; or

- an official stops play due to injured player or because of her or his own illness, injury, or another emergency, or to confer with other officials, or because of an unusual delay in putting the ball back into play.

When officials stop play because of an injury, they should wait until the ball becomes dead or until it's being controlled by the team of the injured player, or at a point where the other team has finished a play. This means that they usually won't stop play while the other team has the ball. They do this to prevent players from faking injuries to stall a fast breaking opponent.

But if an injury is serious enough, an official may suspend play under any circumstances to protect the injured player and get him or her immediate medical attention.

If time is called for an injury, no time-out will be charged if the injured player is able to get right back in play or is immediately replaced. There's also no time-out if a player needs to retrieve their glasses or a lost contact lens.

TIME-OUT

Any player can ask the official for a time-out. However, don't ask for a time-out if the other team has the ball.

You are entitled to a time-out if:

• your team has the ball (but not during a loose ball or after your team scores a basket);

• the ball is dead (but not when the other team is throwing the ball in);

• a disqualified or injured player has been replaced; or

• the scorer signals that a correctable error has been made and the referee stops play to correct it.

CHARGED TIME-OUT

Under NCAA rules, a time-out lasts 75 seconds. There will be a warning signal after 60 seconds, and at the end of the 75 seconds, a signal to resume play. Players may not be substituted between that 60- and 75-second period. If play is not resumed immediately at the 75-second signal, the team will be charged another, 75-second time-out. Or, if one team is ready and the other is stalling or moving too slowly back onto the court, play may be started with just the one team.

When your team has been given a time-out, it's not necessary that you use up the entire 75 seconds. The captain should let the official know that they are finished. Why give the time to your opponents if you are ready? Seventy-five seconds is not a very long time. Hustle over and listen. The coach will probably have a lot to say in that small bit of time.

NUMBER OF TIME-OUTS

Because many people's exposure to basketball is limited to televised NCAA games, they may think that each team has three time-outs. A team is entitled to *five* time-outs during a normal game. But when a game is being broadcast on TV (and has time-outs for commercials) three time-outs per team for men are allowed. In case of tied games, each team gets one time-out per overtime period.

If a team doesn't use their time-outs, they can be rolled over to the next time period, including overtimes.

If a team needs more than the allotted number of time-outs after they've used theirs up, they can have them—at a cost. Each extra time-out will cost the team a technical foul. As an individual player, you should stay aware of the number of time-outs your team has used and how many are left. Calling a time-out when you don't have one could cost you the game.

STARTING THE CLOCK

When the ball is thrown in, the clock starts when the ball touches a player on the court. The shot clock starts when one team gains control of the ball on court. When a free throw is being taken, the clock starts when *the ball is touched* after the shot is missed, or when it's thrown in bounds after a score.

OVERTIME

If the score is tied at the end of the second half, the game is extended. After a one-minute break, play continues for five more minutes; after that, if the score is still tied, you play five more minutes, and five more after that if necessary. There's no limit to how many overtime periods can be played. The record number of overtimes in Division I NCAA play is seven, which occurred on December 21, 1981. The participants were the University of Cincinatti and Bradley University. Cincinatti won 75-73.

Chapter 4

Violations

FLOOR VIOLATIONS

A floor violation is an infraction that a player commits in handling the ball or taking a position on the court—but one that does not endanger or impede another player.

Floor violation penalty

When the floor violations that have been listed in this chapter are committed, the ball's dead and will quickly be awarded to a nearby opponent. The referee will indicate the spot just off the court where your opponents throw the ball in.

TRAVELING

Traveling is walking or running while holding on to the ball. If you travel, the other team will be given the ball. However, when holding the ball, you may pivot on one foot. After you have established your pivot foot, make sure not to lift that foot off the floor. This sounds simple, but there's a little more to it than that.

If you catch the ball while you're running or beginning or ending a dribble, there are very exact rules on how your pivot foot is established and what you may do with it:

 • If you're in the air and catch the ball, then land on both feet at once, either foot may pivot.

• If you land on both feet but one comes down first, the one down first has to be the pivot.

• If you come down only on one foot, and the other doesn't come down, you may jump and land on both feet, but now you no longer may pivot.

If you hold the ball and pivot:

• When your pivot foot leaves the floor (if you jump, for example) you must let go of the ball. That is, you must pass or shoot before your foot comes down, or you will be called for traveling.

If you catch the ball, pivot, and then want to dribble, make sure you release the ball into the dribble before you lift your pivot foot.

If you stop under circumstances where you can't pivot:

• You may lift either or both feet, but you can't legally bring them back down; you must pass or shoot the ball before you do or you'll be called for traveling.

• If you fall while holding the ball, you will find it impossible not to lift your feet and will almost certainly be called for traveling.

29

DOUBLE DRIBBLE

By the rules, a dribble is the action of pushing, patting, tapping, or batting the ball to the ground with one hand and the ball returning to one hand (either left or right), once or repeatedly. The ball can bounce on the floor more than once before it returns to your hand, but it must touch the floor at least once—you may not "dribble" the ball off your knees, the ceiling, or the heads of your teammates. You may only dribble *once* while you've got the ball. Your dribble is finished and you may not resume it when:

- the ball stops moving or rests in *one* or *both* of your hands;

- you touch the ball with both of your hands at once;

When your dribble ends and you are still in control of a live ball, you must either pass the ball or shoot.

A double dribble will not be called on you if you resume your dribble after:

- a try for a field goal;

- the ball has been batted free by an opponent;

- a pass or fumble where the ball gets touched by another player; or

- the ball is whistled dead.

30

1...2...3...

THREE-SECOND RULE

If there weren't some restrictions on offensive players in the free throw lane, what you'd see would start to resemble the line of scrimmage at a football game more than a basketball competition.

If your team has the ball in the frontcourt, you must keep moving. Don't camp out under the basket. If you spend any longer than three seconds in the free throw lane, you could be called for a violation (the restraining circle around the free throw line does not count). If you've been in the lane less than three seconds, get the ball and then start a move to the hoop, you won't be called for a violation, even if you take longer than three seconds in the lane. But you must shoot, or it is a violation, and the ball will be turned over to your opponents.

TEN-SECOND RULE

In NCAA men's play one team can't retain control of the ball in the backcourt for more than 10 seconds or it will be turned over to their opponents. A team has ten seconds from the time the ball is thrown in bounds to move the ball up into the frontcourt. This rule not only keeps up the pace of the game, but encourages aggressive, full-court defense, making the game more interesting and balanced. Remember, if you are bringing the ball up against a full-court defense and there's a scramble for the ball, the ref is still counting off your ten seconds. If you regain control, you'll probably have to hurry to get across the "time line."

BACKCOURT

FRONTCOURT

FRONTCOURT   BACKCOURT

32

Once your team has managed to move the ball into the frontcourt, you can't retreat into your backcourt to stall or spread the defense. A backcourt violation will be called. You'll lose the ball if you or your teammates in the backcourt even touch the ball when you've already advanced it to the frontcourt. Of course, if a defensive player deflects a pass or knocks it out of your hands and into the backcourt, you're free to run it down and play it without a backcourt violation being called. And if you have a throw-in from the midcourt stripe—say, following a held ball—you can make the throw to a teammate in your backcourt without committing a violation.

FRONTCOURT

FRONTCOURT

FIVE SECONDS CLOSELY GUARDED

If you are in the frontcourt, holding the ball and you are closely guarded by an opponent (6 feet is considered close), you have five seconds to do something with the ball. You're not allowed to simply stand there protecting the ball from the defender.

6 FT.

ELBOWS

Be careful with your arms and elbows. It's okay to move your arms in ways that are related to the total movement of your body, in running, catching, or releasing the ball.

KICKED BALL

Don't kick the ball. A "kick" is any *intentional* strike by your knee or any part of your leg or foot below your knee. If a defensive player kicks the ball, the offense will take the ball out of bounds with the clock reset. Also, don't strike the ball with your fist.

BASKET INTERFERENCE AND GOALTENDING

Every coach could prevent opponents from scoring by stationing a player with good jumping ability near the basket to swat shots away that are dropping into the basket. Even a stocky five-footer could stand right under the basket and poke balls back out through the top as they were dropping in. The problem is, if these tactics were legal the score for most games would be 6-4 after 40 minutes, and that's not basketball.

There are very definite ways in which you are not allowed to interfere with a shot. What you may or may not do to stop the ball from entering the basket is determined by the ball's position in relation to the basket and to the cylinder of space above it. Just imagine that the basket is a spotlight sending a beam of light straight up above it. You must be careful what you do near this cylindrical "beam." Here's what the rules say:

- Once the ball is on the rim or in the basket, don't touch it. The ball is considered to be in the basket when any part of it dips below the level of the hoop.

- Don't touch a ball that's partially or completely in the cylinder above the basket.

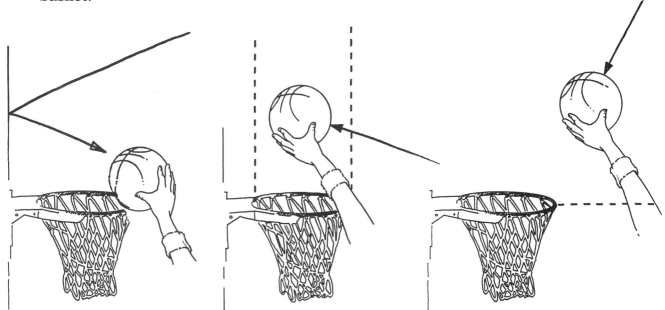

- Don't reach through the basket from below and touch the ball in or outside the cylinder.

- Don't touch a ball that either was shot toward the basket for a field goal, or tapped toward the basket, if it is:

  1) on its way down; *and*
  2) entirely above the level of the rim; *and*
  3) might, by any stretch of the imagination, go in.

If you do, you will be called for goaltending.

LEGAL BLOCK

If you are guilty of goaltending or basket interference at your opponent's basket, the penalty is:

- during a two-point field goal attempt, the other team is awarded **two points**;

- during a three-point field goal attempt, **three points**; and

- during a free throw attempt, **one point.**

If you commit the violation at your own basket, any basket scored will not count and the ball will be given to your opponents.

Now, even if you were to do the first two things listed here—touch the rim or a ball while it's inside the cylinder—it's okay *if and only if* you had your hand on the ball beforehand, and you kept your hand on the ball entered the basket cylinder. In other words, it's okay if you are dunking the ball or your hand was forced into that position while trying to prevent a dunk.

Chapter 5

Fouls

Fouls fall into two main categories: personal and technical. **Personal fouls** are committed when the ball is live. A personal foul involves some kind of illegal contact among the players: A player has touched, pushed, or bumped against another player in a way that gives an unfair advantage or could cause injury. **Technical fouls** are usually "etiquette" or procedural violations—misbehavior or errors by players or team personnel that interfere with the fair play of the game. Any fouls committed by nonplayers are technicals. Technical fouls also include contact fouls committed by players on the court when the ball is dead.

PERSONAL FOULS

You are permitted to confuse and intimidate your opponents, or disrupt their game plan. In fact, you should try to! But you are *not* permitted to hold, push, charge, or trip your opponents. Nor are you permitted to extend your arms, shoulders, hips, knees, or contort any part of your body to physically restrain your opponent, whether the player you are guarding has the ball or not. Although officials are only human and they never catch every infraction, the list of what you may not do is fairly explicit. These forbidden actions are called personal fouls.

LEGAL USE OF HANDS AND ARMS

You're not allowed to grab hold of other players or their uniforms for any reason. The rules state that you are not supposed to contact them with your hands at all, even if it's just a touch to help you sense where they are. But this sort of contact is usually overlooked by officials.

And in going for a steal or trying to block a shot, it's not a foul if your hand hits an opponent's hand holding the ball. Technically, the opponent's hand is considered an extension of the ball. But most officials call a foul if they spot any contact in this situation.

When guarding an opponent, it's a good idea to extend your limbs and make yourself look big to cut down the opposing team's options. It *is* legal to extend your elbows out in a natural way, just as it is when you are rebounding, setting a screen, or when blocking under the basket, but don't flail in such an uncontrolled way that you pick up a personal foul. Don't extend your arms to hinder your opponent's bodily freedom of movement. You may, however, hold your hands up in front of your face to protect yourself or take the impact of collision or charge.

41

Don't push. Anytime a defensive player makes jarring contact with the ball handler from behind, even if the dribbler stops suddenly, that's viewed as a push. If you give another player "the hip" in a way that delays and hinders them from moving, that's blocking.

Similarly, when you are handling the ball, you may not use your forearms or hands to ward off an opponent when you are dribbling or shooting. If you are caught doing this, you will be called for a foul.

43

VERTICALITY

In defending against an opponent, you may jump as high and as often as you want, as long as the movement is *vertical*, and you may raise your hands and arms vertically, up and over your head, without being penalized. But if you are leaning or reaching over your opponent and he or she goes up to shoot, you will almost certainly be called for a foul. Think of your vertical plane as all the space that extends straight up—but not out—from you.

The offensive player—if you are legally guarding him—is not allowed to contact you, by jumping at you or pushing. If he does, he will be called for a foul.

CHARGING

Even if you are concentrating on controlling or receiving a pass, you must still keep your head up and avoid committing a personal foul. Don't dribble through, run over, or back into players in your path. Also, don't try to force your way through opposing players by dribbling or running between them where there's no room for you.

If you go by one of your opponents so that at least your head and shoulders have moved past his, then it becomes your opponent's responsibility to avoid a contact foul.

If, as you move forward without the ball, you get momentum going in a straight line, a defender can't crowd you out of the path you have established. But if he has a legal defensive position in that path and has given you a few step's worth of space, you must go around him.

DRAWING A CHARGE

Many players intentionally position themselves so that their opponents will run into them and be called for charging. Remember these points when you are trying to "draw a charge":

• If you are in a legal stance, and the player driving with the ball runs into you, the other player will be called for a charge and forfeit the ball.

• There is no specific distance you must keep to make sure a dribbler has time to maneuver.

• Once an opponent with the ball leaves the ground, it's too late to shuffle over and assume a legal position. You must be in your legal guarding position before he makes his move.

• Keep your body facing the player you are guarding, and plant both your feet on the floor.

46

AVOIDING FOULS WHEN SCREENING

When on offense, there are certain ways in which you are allowed to make yourself into a barrier or screen.

• When setting a screen behind an opponent, stay at least two steps from them.

• When you are at their side or front where they can see you if they look, you can set the screen as close as you like.

• When the player you are screening is moving at high speed down court, don't step in front of them so that they're forced into a collision. They must have enough time to change direction. It's up to you to estimate the player's speed and set the screen far enough away—one, two strides, or more—for him or her to avoid a collision.

• If you are the defensive player and you are behind your opponent moving along in the same path and direction, you are the one responsible for preventing contact. If he or she slows down and you collide, it's your fault.

• Once you're in a legal screening position, don't shift until the play is complete. As we mentioned earlier, you can't bodily force an opponent out of his path by mirroring his motions—that is, by creating a "moving screen."

It's okay, when you are screening a player, to line up next to other screening teammates, but make sure to keep your "double screen" at least 6 feet from the nearest boundary. Building a human fortress around one player is not basketball, and this rule is designed to prevent that from happening.

Players who are being screened may not run over their opponents. If you're being screened and you can see the player who is screening you, you must try to avoid excessive contact by going around the screener. Don't use your hands, arms, hips, or shoulders to shove your way around a screen or to hold or push away the screener. But if you accidentally make contact, even hard contact, with a blind screen, it's okay.

FLAGRANT FOULS

A flagrant personal foul is defined in the rules as the use of any body part in a way that endangers other players. Crouching under another player, punching another player, or forcing someone to flip over you would be good examples.

Some flagrant fouls pass over the line into fights. There are harsh penalties for fighting—ejection from a game or suspension for the entire season. An official can invoke penalties for fighting anytime there is any kind of hitting or overt, combative behavior. Kicking or throwing punches, whether or not any of the punches or kicks land, are obvious examples. If you do something so unsporting that your opponent retaliates by fighting, there's a good chance you'll be penalized as the instigator of the fight.

INTENTIONAL FOULS

These can be called as personal or as technical fouls. An intentional foul is seen as occurring not as a normal part of play, but deliberately. Not, "Oops, I fouled him trying to get the ball," but, "I'll foul him if that's the only way I can stop the clock" (or the shot or whatever). The presence of intention is key; it doesn't matter how heinous the infraction or how minor—if you obviously meant to do it, it's an intentional foul.

The ref will particularly be looking for a player who:

- holds or pushes a player with the purpose of stopping the play; or

- pushes or grabs a player in the back to stop him from scoring when there's no chance this was done to guard him.

You are also guilty of an intentional foul if you:

- make contact with a player who is throwing the ball in.

The penalty for any of these is two free throws, and the ball out of bounds.

51

PENALTIES FOR PERSONAL FOULS

No free throws are awarded for common fouls or player-control fouls (ones committed by the player with the ball), for example, illegal screens or charges. Instead, the team that was fouled is given the ball to throw in bounds.

But if your team commits a total of six personal fouls during one half, then for the seventh foul—and every foul after that—your opponents get a free throw and if they make it, they get an additional bonus throw.

Finally, if the members of the team together commit more than nine of these fouls, then for the tenth foul, and every foul after that—of any kind except player control—the other team will get two free throws. This "double bonus" is true *only* in NCAA men's basketball. It is not true in NCAA women's, high school, or junior high basketball.

Along with the free throws that are awarded for each foul, there's a cumulative penalty: If a player commits a total of five fouls (personal, unsporting, contact technical, or flagrant) over the course of play, that player is out of the game—disqualified.

If a team is "in the bonus," or fouled when shooting, they are awarded a free throw or throws. Successful free throws count one point each. The rules that determine how many shots you get are as follows:

One free throw is awarded to you:

- if you were fouled while trying for a field goal, but you made the goal anyway (even if it's a three-point shot); or

- for each multiple foul committed against you, you get one throw for each nonflagrant foul.

Two free throws are awarded to you:

- if a player fouls you while you are shooting, and you miss the shot;

- if a player intentionally or flagrantly fouls you (after the free throws, the ball is awarded out of bounds to your team at the spot the foul occurred);

- if another player commits a flagrant technical foul (after the throws, your team will also get the ball in bounds to be taken at one end of the division line);

- if multiple fouls are committed against you, and any of the fouls are intentional or flagrant (again, your team gets the ball for a throw in when the free throws are completed).

Three free throws are awarded to you:

- if your opponent fouls you while you are attempting a three-point basket and you don't make the basket. If the foul against you was intentional or flagrant, your team will also get the ball inbounds at the division line.

A multiple personal foul is called when two or more opponents foul you at the same time. One shot is awarded for each nonflagrant foul and two shots for each flagrant foul. A **double personal foul** is when two opponents commit common fouls against each other more or less at the same time. Double fouls are resolved by the alternating-possession process.

TECHNICAL FOULS

Technical fouls are noncontact or procedural fouls committed by players, the bench, or staff. Technicals are also called for contact fouls committed while the ball is dead.

   Your team can get a technical foul even before the game starts. If your side delays the beginning of the game by a minute or more, or if you don't get the roster to the scorer before the game, it's a technical foul against your team. Your team can get technicals for illegally changing the starting lineup or squad lists. (These points are covered in more detail in Chapter 2.) During the game, if your team stays in a huddle too long or in any other way delays a throw-in or free throw, or takes too many time-outs, that's a technical foul.

Other technical fouls are:

- having too many players on the court;

- batting the ball after your team scores or holding the ball to prevent your opponents from putting it quickly into play. This is most commonly done to buy time for the defense to set up and prevent a quick fast-break basket. (After your team has scored, just let the ball drop, don't touch it or impede your opponent, who wants to throw it in, from getting the ball);

Also, individual players can get technicals if they:

- stay on the court after being disqualified;

- dunk a dead ball; or

- intentionally strike or shake the backboard or rim while a shot is being attempted, while the ball is in or on the basket, or while the ball is in the cylinder of space above the rim.

One kind of technical is a personal-contact foul that occurs when the ball is dead—for example, pushing an opponent while setting up on the foul line before a free throw. When this occurs during the maneuvers that generally occur before a throw-in, it's just a personal foul.

54

UNSPORTING CONDUCT

The rules state that players are expected to behave in a fair, ethical, and honorable fashion. Intentionally shooting foul shots that should be shot by a teammate is unsporting. Dishonesty is against the rules, and the culprit is guilty of an unsporting foul.

Remember, one of the dictionary definitions of the word "sport" is "a person who is sportsmanlike, easygoing, companionable." Act that way. You don't have to keep your hair combed or a smile on your face, but try to behave in a manner that you will be proud of when thinking back over the game.

A player might be called for an unsporting foul if he or she:

- taunts, teases, points at, ridicules, or uses obscene language or gestures to another player;

- uses hands to block an opponent's vision near their eyes; or

55

● grasps the basket, except to prevent injury to himself or another player.

● shows disrespect to officials (You don't have to use explicitly vulgar language to get a technical called on you. For players or nonplayers, merely expressing resentment in the way you address, contact, or gesture to an offical is prohibited.)

Though these don't occur often, here are a few other things that can earn you a technical:

● touching the ball during a free throw flight;

● leaving the court without permission;

● delaying returning to the court when you've been out of bounds;

● wearing an illegal shirt or number;

● when substituting, not having your name on the squad list, not reporting to the scorers, and not waiting for the official to beckon you.

TECHNICALS BY NONPLAYERS

Finally, these things may not be done in the bench area:

Except for the head coach, team personnel should stay seated when the clock is running and the ball is live. Leaping to your feet to cheer is okay, but sit right back down.

Generally speaking, the rules require staff and nonplaying squad members to stay on the bench or in the coach's box during the game.

Most referees don't want to mar the game by calling silly and unnecessary technicals—and the coach will not be held inside the box as if it were a cage. They will look the other way for behavior that could be called a technical foul but would sour the spirit of the contest if they called it. But *technically*, "in the coach's box," as with other boundary lines, means not even touching the boundary lines. There are, however, a couple of exceptions.

Head coaches and other coaches, attendants, and personnel may leave the box area to get information from a scorer or timer during an intermission or time-out. A coach, trainer, or team physician may also, with permission, come onto the court to check on a seriously injured player. Players may leave only to report to the scorer's table.

Also, it's okay for any team personnel to go over to the scorers or timers to point out a mistake they may have made or to request a time-out for a correctable error. However, be warned that if you are wrong and there was no mistake (or the error was *not* correctable), a time-out will be charged to your team.

57

The other exception has to do with fighting. If a fight breaks out or is about to, the head coach may leave the bench area to help break it up. If *anyone else* leaves, they will be disqualified and must either go to the locker room or leave the building altogether.

Anytime any coach, player on the bench, or any team attendant or assistant does any of the following, they may earn their team a technical foul:

- try to affect how an official makes a call;

- bait or address an official or opponent with disrespect;

- curse;

- object to an official's decision, even by only rising from the bench and/or gesturing;

- throw debris on the court;

- enter the court without authorization;

They also may not:

- incite unruly behavior in the crowd;

- fail to promptly replace a player who must be replaced (it should be done within 30 seconds if a sub is available);

- engage in any unsporting behavior;

- use whistles, electronic equipment, sound-making devices, or megaphones for courtside coaching; or

- refuse the bench that is assigned.

PENALTIES FOR TECHNICAL FOULS

When a technical foul is called on a team, the other team gets two free throws. After the throws, the nonoffending team also gets a throw-in at midcourt.

Any contact, technical, or unsporting fouls count in the total of five fouls you are allowed per game. Any technical fouls committed by any of the nonplaying team personnel count towards the team totals *and* against the head coach personally. More than two technicals against a coach personally or three against the coach's team (including ones called on the coach), and he is disqualified and ejected from the game.

FIGHTING

Fighting is considered a flagrant foul. In college, the first time in a season that you have a foul called on you for fighting and you are ejected, part of the penalty above and beyond that for a flagrant foul is that you may not play in the next game. The second time in the season, and you are out for the season, including any tournament play. If you are suspended for fighting, whether for the game or the season, you may not even sit on the bench.

Chapter 6

Out of Bounds and Throw-Ins

THE BOUNDARIES

In the first chapter, there was a diagram showing the different areas and boundaries that make up a basketball court. The game must be played inside the boundaries of the court. That means *inside* the lines—the boundary-marking lines themselves are out of bounds. If you touch those lines, or the floor outside them, or any object or person out of bounds, then you are out of bounds.

In Chapter 1, we saw how a player's status—in-bounds or out-of-bounds, frontcourt or backcourt—is decided by where the player is contacting or had last contacted the floor. Remember, too, that the ball's status when it touches an

official is determined by where the official is touching the ground. If the ball touches *any* person or object that is out, the ball is out. This includes the backboard supports and the back but not the edge of the backboard, the ceiling, and anything hanging from or connected to the ceiling. The ball is also out of bounds if it passes over the backboard from any direction.

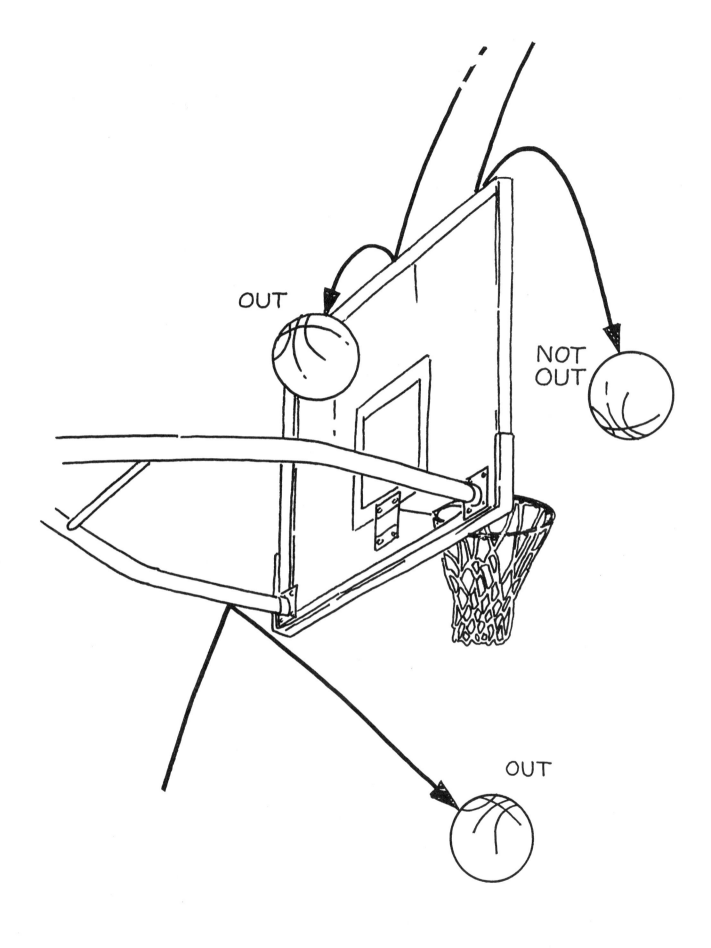

OUT

NOT
OUT

OUT

If you are on court and you are the last player to touch it, *or to be touched by it*, before it goes out, then the ball is awarded to your opponents. If it goes out because of touching something other than a player, or touches you while you are standing out, you still "caused" it to go out—at least for purposes of determining the throw-in.

Sometimes the officials simply don't agree *who* made the ball go out, or maybe two players touched the ball and simultaneously sent it out. In these cases, the alternating-possession rule determines who throws the ball in.

AWARDED THROW-INS

A throw-in will be awarded:

- after a field goal or a successful free throw if it is the last or only free throw to be awarded;

- after a player-control foul, or a common foul before the bonus is in effect;

- after a lane violation or other free throw violation by the team at the line with one foul shot;

- after a held ball (if the alternating-possession rule is in effect);

- after a free throw has been taken for a technical foul, the throw-in will be made by the team that shot the free throws and will be made at the division line (any player can do this); or

- if the ball becomes dead while one team is in control, but not because of a foul and not because time has expired.

There are some differences in the way throw-ins are made after a score compared to the way they are made after violations or out-of-bounds calls.

When throwing the ball in *after a goal is scored,* you may throw the ball from a standing position, as is most commonly done. But you may also move along the endline or pass the ball to another teammate out of bounds and allow them to throw it. *After a violation or out-of-bounds* call, you may not leave the throw-in spot designated by the official and the designated player must throw the ball in.

After a technical foul the throw-in is made at the midcourt line, on either side, and may be thrown to a teammate in either the front or backcourt without danger of a backcourt violation.

67

PUTTING THE BALL IN PLAY

To put the ball in play after a player causes it to go out of bounds, or after a foul occurs, the ref hands the ball to a player from the nonoffending team. Usually, the next step is for this player to throw it in from a spot near where the ball went out or the foul was committed. However, if this spot is behind the backboard—because, for example, the ball went out right under the basket—then the throw-in may be made from a spot out of bounds and aligned with the outside of free throw lane.

You have five seconds to throw the ball in or the throw will go to the other team. You must throw the ball, not hand it to another player or carry it onto the court. To throw it in, it's okay to jump up or move back, but not to run or jump

1, 2, 3, 4, 5,

O.K.

NOT
O.K.

sideways. Although it's okay to touch the boundary with your foot, it's not okay to step over the line. So it's a good policy not to touch or lean over the boundary line toward the court.

Make sure you pass the ball directly into the court so that the first thing it touches is the floor in-bounds or a teammate. Don't bounce it first, and don't throw it at the basket, backboard, ceiling, or anything else except a teammate. If a throw-in lodges on the rim, the ball will go to the other team to be thrown in.

In defending against a throw-in, remember that if you attempt to reach for the ball in your opponent's hands, you'll be called for a technical foul.

Chapter 7

Field Goals and Free throws

SCORING

One universal truth in team sports is that the team with the best score wins. In basketball, you score points when you make a basket—that is, you put the ball all the way through the basket from the top. The clock must be running when you make your shot; specifically, for the basket to count the clock must be running at the instant the ball leaves your hand. But if the game clock or the shot clock runs out while your shot is passing through the air and into the basket, it's a legal goal.

Depending on circumstances, a basket can be worth one, two, or three points.

Every free throw you make will give your team one point.

Most goals made from the court during play count two points for your team—provided you put them in your team's basket. It will count for the other guys if it ricochets off your head and goes in their basket.

You may not score a goal by shooting the ball into the basket when making a throw-in. Nor can you score by throwing the ball up through the bottom of the hoop and letting it drop back through.

If you can score from beyond the three-point line, your shot is worth three points. Caution: When you start to shoot a three-pointer, you must have at least one foot on the floor behind and not touching this line and neither foot touching or inside the arc. If you jump from beyond the three-point line, though, it doesn't matter where you land—it's still a three-pointer if you make it.

How can you score without the ball going through the basket? Your team is awarded points when your opponents commit either a goaltending or a basket interference infraction. (These infractions are discussed on page 37.)

WHO TAKES THE FREE THROW

If a personal foul was committed against you and free throws are awarded, then *you* must take them. If you were injured on the play, then the substitute that is sent in to take your place must take the throw. For technical fouls, the captain of your team designates who the free thrower will be—probably the best free throw shooter on the team—and the captain is free to designate the newly substituted player. (See the section on substitutions in Chapter 2.)

THE FREE THROW PROCEDURE

Your teammates and the players from the other team take alternate positions in the four marked lane spaces on either side of the free throw lane. These eight players create a sort of alley between you and the basket. They must stand one player per space, with your opponents in the spaces nearest the basket (and only those two slots must be filled.) Any players not in lane spaces must be behind the free throw line and behind the three-point line.

Once you have the ball, your opponents are not allowed to try to rattle or startle you. And none of the other players may:

- enter or leave the lane spaces;

- step into the lane to rebound before the ball has left the shooter's hand;

- occupy spaces along the lane that should go to a member of the other team; or

74

• move from their place until the ball hits the rim if they aren't stationed on the free throw lane but on the court behind you;

When you are shooting technical, intentional or flagrant fouls, the other players don't take places on the lane—you're going to get the ball out of bounds anyway so there's no reason to station rebounders under the basket. The other players must all stand outside the three-point arc and behind the free throw line.

PENALTIES

If you or anyone on your team makes a lane violation when you are shooting a free throw, your score won't count. If it's your last shot, the ball will be awarded to the other team. If someone on the other team commits a violation but you make your shot anyway, there's no penalty to the other team. If you don't score, however, you are permitted to take your throw again.

MAKING A LEGAL FREE THROW

The rules cover all elements of the free throw itself, and these rules carry their own violations.

First and foremost, when making a free throw, stay behind the line and don't touch the line with your foot. You must stand within the half-circle of the free throw area. Once you have the ball in your hands:

- you have *only ten seconds* to make one throw. If you have two throws, you'll have ten seconds for the second throw as well;

1, 2, 3, 4, 5, 6, 7, 8, 9, 10

● don't fake a throw and then shoot in an attempt to get a lane violation called
if you miss; and

● wait to cross the free throw line until the ball has struck the rim or
backboard. (The idea is to prevent you from tossing hard free throws, getting
your own rebound, and then attempting to score two points instead of one.)

Unless you are shooting technicals, after a *successful* single or second free throw (there's not another throw to be tried), your opponents use a throw-in to get the ball back into play.

The procedure is different if you *miss* your final free throw, even if you made the first one. For unsuccessful tries, the ball simply goes live again. Now all those players who lined up along the lane will go for the rebound as play resumes.

LEARN HOW TO PLAY ANY SPORT

SPORTS RULES IN PICTURES

__BASEBALL RULES IN PICTURES
by G. Jacobs and J. R. McCrory   0-399-51597-6/$8.95

__BASKETBALL RULES IN PICTURES
edited by A. G. Jacobs   0-399-51842-8/$8.95

__FOOTBALL RULES IN PICTURES
edited by Don Schiffer and Lud Duroska   0-399-51689-1/$8.95

__GOLF RULES IN PICTURES
by The U.S. Golf Association   0-399-51799-5/$10.00

__HOCKEY RULES IN PICTURES
by The National Hockey League   0-399-51772-3/$8.95

__OFFICIAL LITTLE LEAGUE BASEBALL
RULES IN PICTURES   0-399-51531-3/$8.95

SPORTS TECHNIQUES IN PICTURES

__BASEBALL TECHNIQUES IN PICTURES
by Michael Brown   0-399-51798-7/$8.95

__FOOTBALL TECHNIQUES IN PICTURES
by Michael Brown   0-399-51769-3/$8.95

__GOLF TECHNIQUES IN PICTURES
by Michael Brown   0-399-51664-6/$10.00